Easy Crochet Slippers

Crochet Slipper Patterns to Make for Adults!

Copyright © 2023

All rights reserved.

DEDICATION

The author and publisher have provided this e-book to you for your personal use only. You may not make this e-book publicly available in any way. Copyright infringement is against the law. If you believe the copy of this e-book you are reading infringes on the author's copyright, please notify the publisher at: https://us.macmillan.com/piracy

Contents

Sunday Ballet Slippers 1

Magic Rectangle Slippers 10

Cloud 9 Slippers 21

Magic Slippers 28

1.5 Hour Slipper 38

Heart & Sole Slippers 52

Shell Slipper 66

Easy Crochet Slippers

Sunday Ballet Slippers

MATERIALS:

Worsted weight/size 4/Aran yarn

-approx. 100 – 120 yards for women's US size 7 – 10 (Big Twist "Dark Denim" pictured)

Easy Crochet Slippers

Crochet hook in size D/3.25mm

PATTERN NOTES:

Place first stitch of each row in the same stitch as your chain.

Ch-2 at beginning of round does NOT count as a stitch.

Pattern written in US terms.

Here's a tutorial for the Magic circle. You could also Chain-4, join to first chain to form a circle.

PATTERN:

Round 1: Magic circle, ch-2, 10dc in circle. Join. (10)

Round 2: Ch-2, 2dc in each st around. Join. (20)

Round 3: Ch-2, * dc in first st, 2dc in next * repeat between * * around, join. (30)

Rounds 4 – 9: Ch-2, dc in each st around. Join. (30)

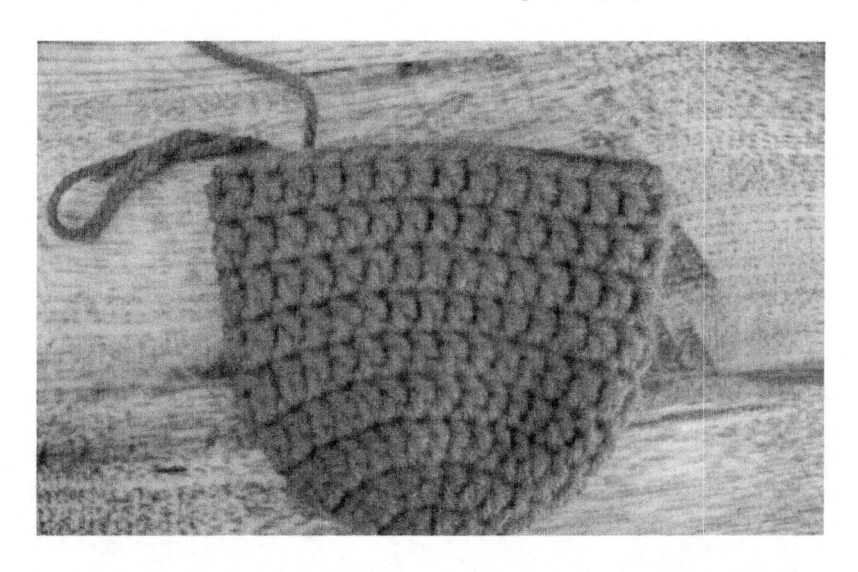

Round 10: Ch-2, dc in 21 sts. ch-2, sc in next 9 sts. Ch-2, sl to top of first dc.

Round 11: Ch-2, dc in 21 sts, ch-4, sc in center 7 sts. Ch-4, sl st to top of first dc.

Round 12: Ch-2, dc in 21 sts, ch-6, sc in center 5 sts. Ch-6, sl st to top of first dc.

Easy Crochet Slippers

Round 13: Ch-2, dc in 21 sts, ch-8, sc in center 3 sts. Ch-8, sl st to top of first dc.

Easy Crochet Slippers

Row 14: Ch-2, dc in 21 sts. (21)

Row 15: Ch-2, turn, 2dc in first, dc in next 19 sts, 2dc in last st (23)

Row 16: ch-2, turn, dc in 23 sts (23)

Row 17: ch-2, turn, 2dc in first, dc in next 21 sts, 2dc in last (25)

Easy Crochet Slippers

Rows 18 – length needed: Ch-2, turn, dc in 25 sts (25)

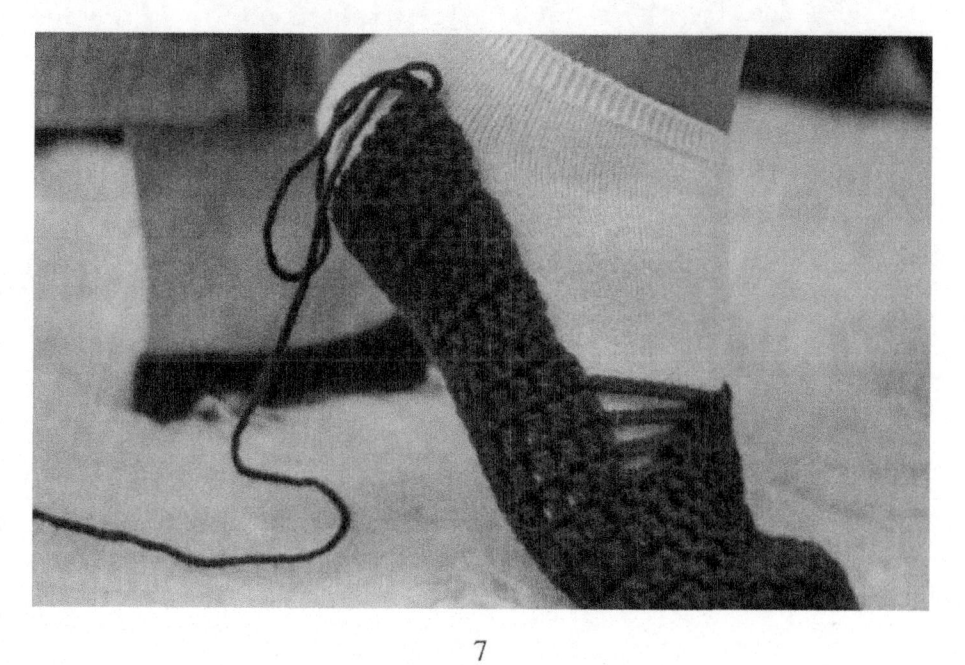

7

stop when slipper length is 1" shorter than foot length

Round 19 (or last row needed for size): Ch-2, turn, dc in 11 sts, dc3tog (middle of heel), dc in 11 sts. Do not fasten off, sl st to top of first st from this row to create the heel. Ch-1, turn if needed.

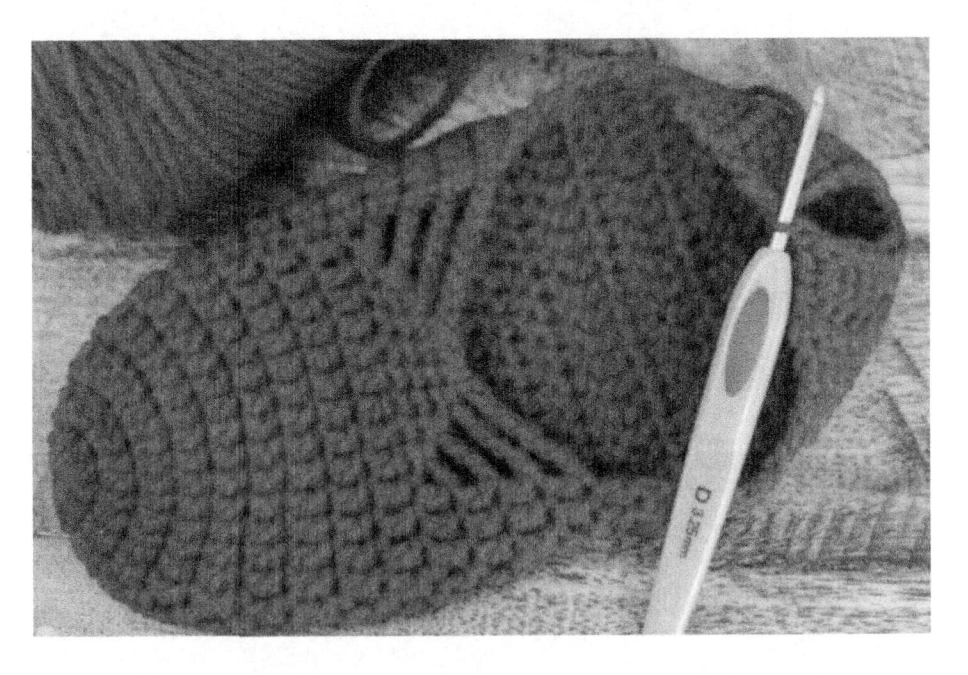

Around top of slipper, with slipper toe facing away from you: sc in each row end until you reach the top of row 14.

Easy Crochet Slippers

Ch-10, sc in center st. Ch-10, sc in top of other side of row 14, sc in each row end to heel.

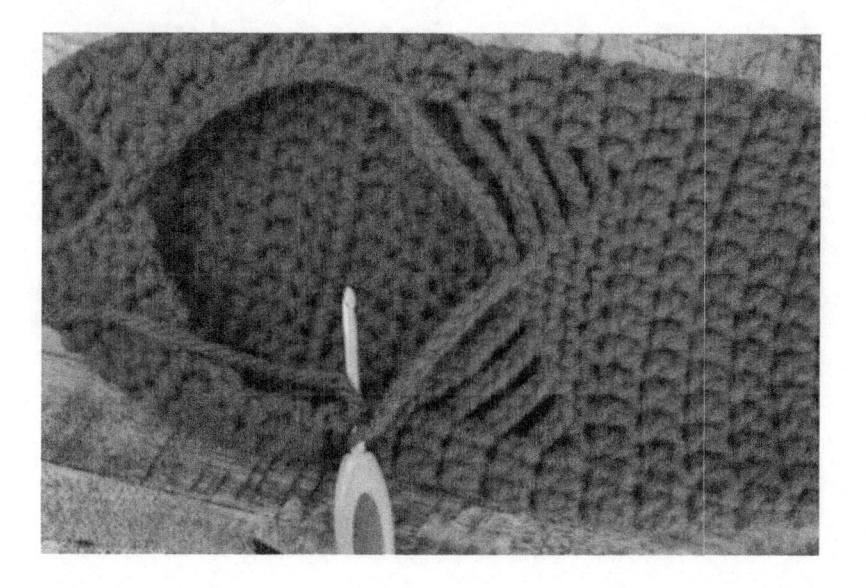

Fasten off and sew down heel using the Mattress Stitch, weave in ends.

Magic Rectangle Slippers

MATERIALS:

A: Lion Brand Wool-Ease Thick & Quick (Weight: 6/super bulky - 106 yds, 6 oz)

Colors pictured:

Easy Crochet Slippers

- Butterscotch [#640-189]

- Succulent (#640-116]

- Oatmeal {#640-123]

- Cilantro [#640-178]

- Clay [#641-102] (available as Bonus Bundle only)

- Tapestry needle

- Size L (8.00 mm) crochet hook or size needed to obtain gauge

- Stitch markers or safety pins

Optional Supplies:

- Leather punch

- Leather or suede for soles

- Small amount of worsted weight yarn in color to match soles

- Monofilament (fishing line)

Easy Crochet Slippers

Gauge:

9 sts x 5.5 rows = 4"

Abbreviations and Glossary (US Terms):

ch – chain

hdc - half double crochet

hdcblo - half double crochet through the back loop only

rep – repeat

st(s) – stitch(es)

Easy Crochet Slippers

Main Rectangle

Notes:

• Ch 1 does not count as a hdc throughout.

• Pattern is written assuming you're using Lion Brand Wool Ease Thick & Quick or similar category 6 yarn. If your yarn weight differs, so will the number of foundation chains you need.

PATTERN:

Foundation Chain: Leaving a long tail on your initial slip knot for seaming later, chain the number of stitches listed in the chart above for the size you're making.

Row 1: Sk first ch, hdc through the back bump of each chain; turn.

The "back bump" is on the underside and looks like a spine running down the chain.

The number of stitches you have now will be one fewer than the number of chains you started with. Each row from here on should contain this number of stitches.

Row 2: Ch 1, hdcblo through the first st and each st to end of row; turn.

"Hdcblo" means you are inserting your hook under the loop that is furthest away from you as you work each stitch.

Row 3: Ch 1, hdcblo through the first st and each st to end of row; turn.

Continue to half double crochet under each loop that is furthest away from you even when you turn your work and begin a new row.

Take a quick minute to measure the width of your rectangle and make sure it's on track to meet the dimensions listed in the table above. If your rectangle is significantly narrower than expected, increase your hook size and try again. If your rectangle significantly wider than expected, reduce your hook size or deliberately work your stitches tighter and try again.

CHECK WIDTH AFTER 2-3 ROWS

Row 4 and Beyond: Repeat Row 3 until piece measures the length of your foot. Fasten off leaving a long tail for seaming.

See table above for length recommendations per size.

Yarn will stretch slightly over time, so resist the urge to extend your rectangle much beyond the length of your foot.

Fasten off leaving a long tail for seaming.

Make a Second Rectangle: Repeat the same steps to make a second identical rectangle. Line rectangles up next to each other and count the visible "bumps" of ribbing to ensure both rectangles have the same number of rows.

Easy Crochet Slippers

PLACING MARKER FOR TOE SEAMING

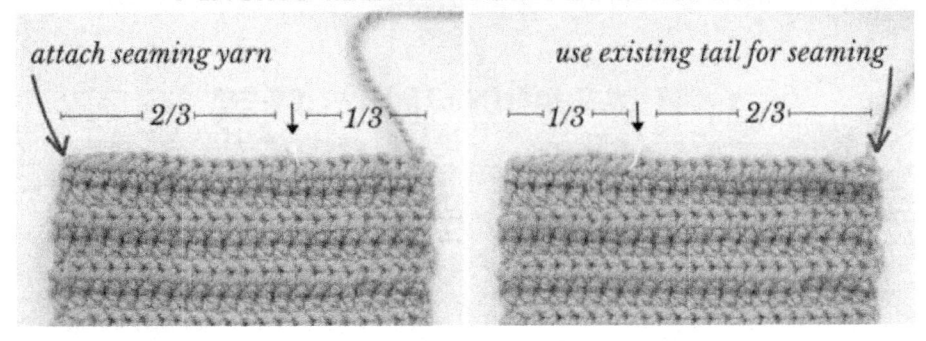

attach seaming yarn — 2/3 — ↓ — 1/3 —   *use existing tail for seaming* — 1/3 — ↓ — 2/3 —

Transforming Rectangles Into Slippers

Notes:

- While finished slippers should be a mirror image of each other, rectangles should be oriented identically to begin the seaming process. (See photo above.)

Toe - Right Slipper

1. Lay rectangle with one tail at top right corner. Divide total number of stitches by 3. Place marker to divide total stitches into a section of 1/3 and 2/3. (See photo above.) If stitch count doesn't cleanly divide by three, place the extra stitch in the shorter section.

2. Using existing tail and tapestry needle, whip stitch in each stitch to marker. Carefully cinch stitches to close toe. It's okay if there is a small opening.

CINCHING TOE CLOSED

A. whip stitch to marker

B. pull to tighten

RIGHT SLIPPER PICTURED

3. Fold remaining ⅓ of rectangle over closed toe. Continuing with same yarn tail and needle, whip stitch across toe.

4. Whip stitch stitch up side of rectangle until slightly less than ½ of edge is seamed down. This can be a good time to try on slipper as you go to achieve desired snugness. While stitching along side, take care to

visually line up rows of ribbing. Fasten off and weave in tail.

Toe - Left Slipper

1. Lay rectangle with tail in top right corner as with right slipper. Use a tapestry needle to weave in this tail as it won't be used.

Counting from the opposite edge you did with the right slipper, place marker to divide rectangle into two sections. (Left slipper marker placement should be a mirror image of right slipper marker placement.)

Attach a new strand of yarn with your tapestry needle in the top left corner. This will serve as your seaming yarn.

Repeat steps 2 through 4 as outlined above.

Easy Crochet Slippers

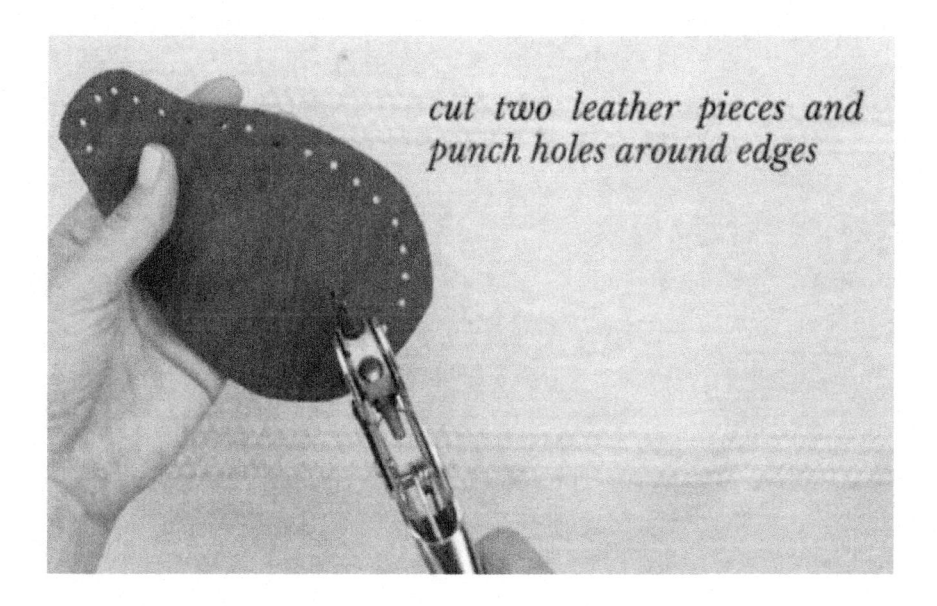

cut two leather pieces and punch holes around edges

Heel - Both Slippers

Using existing yarn tail and tapestry needle, zig zag stitch from top of heel to bottom. Fasten off and weave in tail.

The following instructions assume you're using a two-piece leather sole like the samples.

Use leather punch to punch holes around toe soles approximately ¼" from edge of leather.

Easy Crochet Slippers

Repeat punching process on heel soles taking care to only punch the first 2" of the heel strip.

Use stitch markers to pin soles in place on slippers. Finish punching heel strip once it's clear how far up holes need to be placed.

With a tapestry needle and yarn that matches sole color, whip stitch soles to slippers. For extended durability, try sewing soles on with yarn and a strand of monofilament (fishing line).

Easy Crochet Slippers

Cloud 9 Slippers

MATERIALS:

Bernat Blanket Yarn (175 yards)

N 9.00mm Crochet Hook

Easy Crochet Slippers

Yarn Needle

Plasti Dip Spray

Size(s):

US Women's Shoe Sizes Small 5-7 (Medium 7.5-9, Large 9.5-10.5)

Difficulty:

Intermediate

Stitches:

Slip Stitch (SS) – Insert hook into stitch. Yarn over. Pull through stitch and loop.

Chain (Ch) – Yarn over. Pull through loop.

Single Crochet (Sc) – Insert hook into stitch. Yarn over. Draw up loop. Yarn over. Pull through 2 loops.

Easy Crochet Slippers

Half Double Crochet (Hdc) – Yarn over. Insert hook into stitch. Yarn over. Draw up loop. Yarn over. Pull through 3 loops.

Double Crochet (Dc) – Yarn over. Insert hook into stitch. Yarn over. Draw up loop. Yarn over. Pull through 2 loops. Yarn over. Pull through 2 loops.

Front Post Double Crochet (Fpdc) – Yarn over. Insert hook from back to front around the stitch. Yarn over. Draw up loop. Yarn over. Pull through 2 loops. Yarn over. Pull through 2 loops.

Back Post Double Crochet (Bpdc) – Yarn over. Insert hook from front to back around the stitch. Yarn over. Draw up loop. Yarn over. Pull through 2 loops. Yarn over. Pull through 2 loops.

Special Stitches:

Single Crochet 2 Together (Sc2tog) – Insert hook into stitch. Yarn over. Draw up loop. Insert hook into next stitch. Yarn over. Draw up loop. Yarn over. Pull through all loops on the hook.

Easy Crochet Slippers

Half Double Crochet 3 together (Hdc3tog) – Yarn over. Insert hook into stitch. Yarn over. Draw up loop. Yarn over. Insert hook into next stitch. Yarn over. Draw up loop. Yarn over. Pull through all loops on the hook.

Double Crochet 3 Together (Dc3tog) – *Yarn over. Insert hook into stitch. Yarn over. Draw up loop. Yarn over. Pull through 2 loops.* Repeat from * to * a total of 2 times. Yarn over pull through all loops on the hook.

Notes:

This pattern is worked from the sole up

This pattern is made working in rounds. Don't forget to work in the same stitch as slip stitch to start each round.

For duel colored slippers, change color for Round 3 and Round 9.

(Optional) After making the soles, finish off and spray generously with Plasti Dip Spray to create a non-slip sole.

Easy Crochet Slippers

PATTERN:

Make 2

Ch 15 (17, 19)

Round 1: In 3 Ch from the hook make 2Dc in the same stitch. Dc to the end until 1 Ch remains. In the last Ch make 6Dc. Working around on the other side of the chain, Dc until the last Ch. Made 2Dc in the last Ch. Join with a SS to the first Dc made. 32 (36, 40)

Round 2: Ch 1. Make 2HDC in each of the next two stitches. Hdc 8 (9,10). Dc 3 (4,5). Make 2Dc in each of the next 6 stitches. Dc 3 (4, 5). HDC 8 (9, 10). 2HDC in each of the last 2 stitches. Join with a SS to the first HDC made. 42 (46, 50)

Round 3: Ch 1. In BLO Sc in each stitch all the way around. Join with a SS to the first Sc made. 42 (46, 50)

Easy Crochet Slippers

Round 4: Ch 1. Sc all the way around. Join with a SS to the first Sc made. 42 (46, 50)

Round 5: Ch 1. Sc 12 (14, 16). *Sc2Tog, Sc* Repeat from * to * a total of 6 times. Sc 12 (14, 16). Join with a SS to the first Sc made. 36 (40, 44)

Round 6: Ch 1. Sc 1. Sc2Tog. Sc 8 (10, 12). *Sc2Tog, Sc* Repeat from * to * a total of 5 times. Sc 7 (9, 11). Sc2Tog. Sc 1. Join with a SS to the first Sc made. 29 (33, 37)

Round 7: Ch 1. Sc 1. Sc2Tog. Sc in the next 6 (8, 10) stitches. HDC2TOG. HDC2TOG. DC3TOg. HDC2TOG. HDC2TOG. Sc in the next 6 (8, 10) stitches. Sc2Tog. Sc. Join with a SS to the first Sc made. 21 (25, 29)

Round 8: Ch 1. Sc 9 (11, 13). DC3TOG. Sc 9 (11, 13). Join with a SS to the first Sc made. 19 (23, 27)

Easy Crochet Slippers

For size Small:

Round 9: Ch 2. Dc in same stitch and each stitch around. Join with a SS to the first stitch made. (19)

For sizes Medium and Large:

Round 9: Ch 2. Dc in same stitch. Dc in the next (10, 12) stitches. DC3TOG. Dc to the end. Join with a SS to the first Dc made. (21, 25)

Round 10: *FPDC, BPDC* repeat from * to * all the way around FPDC around the last stitch. Join with a SS to the first FPDC made.

Finish off and weave in your ends.

Easy Crochet Slippers

Magic Slippers

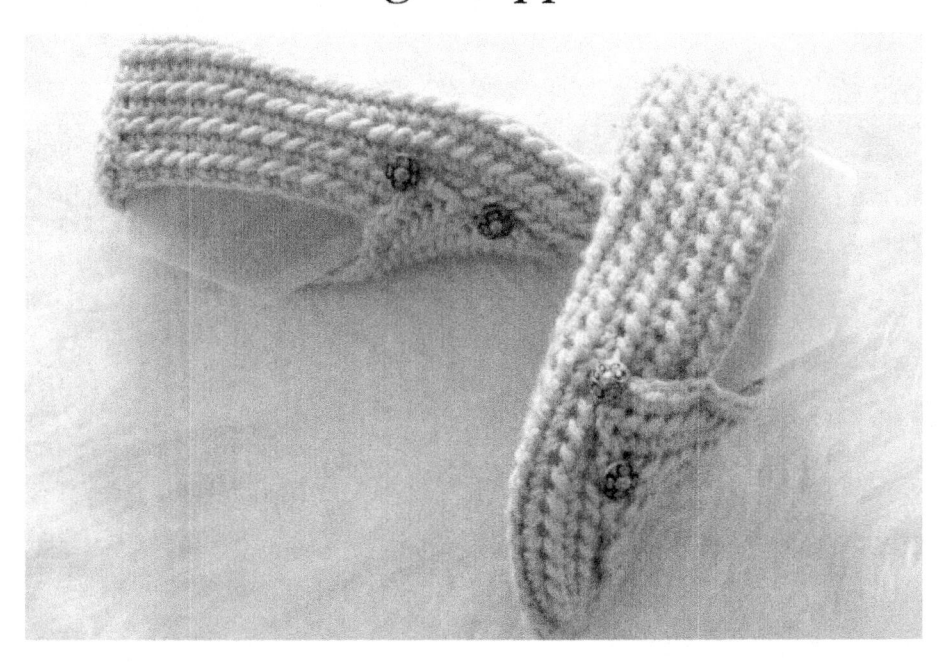

MATERIALS:

1. Size 4 worsted weight yarn. Loops and Threads Impeccable yarn in colors Putty and Barley were used for the sample slippers.

2. Size J(6mm) hook

3. Tapestry needle to weave in the end and shape the slippers

4. Four 3/4-inch metal buttons for embellishment

Easy Crochet Slippers

Finished Size

Note: Sizes are based on US shoe sizes.

Size 5: 8-1/4 inches long

Size 6: 8-3/4 inches long

Size 7: 9 inches long

Size 8: 9-1/4 inches long

Size 9: 9-3/4 inches long

Size 10: 10 inches long

Easy Crochet Slippers

Yardage

Around 160-200 Yards depending on the size you are making.

Stitch Abbreviations

ch-chain

sc-single crochet

hslst- half double crochet slip stitch

YO-yarn over

Gauge

12.5 hslst= 4 inches

Stitch Explanations

Half double crochet slip stitch(hslst): YO, insert your hook into the next st, YO and pull through the stitch and the 2 loops on your hook.

Easy Crochet Slippers

PATTERN:

Note: Stitch counts are given in the order Size 5(6, 7, 8, 9, 10). Alternate numbers have been highlighted for ease.

Ch 26(27, 28, 30, 32, 33)

Row 1: 1 sc in 2nd ch from hook and each ch across to end, turn.——25(26, 27, 29, 31, 32) sts

Row 2: Ch 1 (does not count as a st here and throughout), hslst in same st as ch 1, hslst in each st across to end, turn.——25(26, 27, 29, 31, 32) sts

Row 3: Ch 1 (does not count as a st here and throughout), 1 sc in same st as ch 1, 1 sc in each st across to end, turn.——25(26, 27, 29, 31, 32) sts

Keep repeating Rows 2 and 3 until your rectangle measures 8(8, 8-

1/2, 8-1/2, 9, 9) inches, fasten off with a 1-1/2 yard tail for sewing.

Shaping the Crochet Slippers

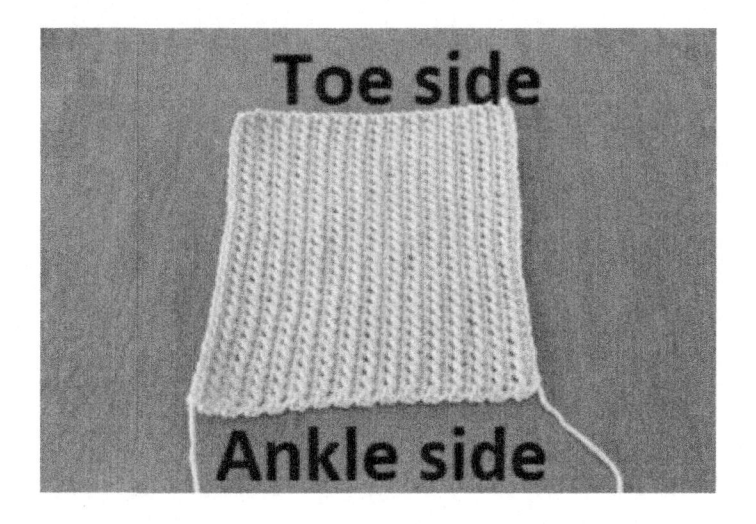

1. The ankle side is where we have the yarn tails

Pattern Notes

The side where you have 2 tails hanging will form the ankle side and the opposite side will form the toe side.

The textured side is the right side of the slipper.

Easy Crochet Slippers

Left Slipper- Cinching Toe Side

Note: You can see the video given at the end.

Keep the rectangle textured side up. The toe side should be at the top.

2. Start from the right side, make a running stitch along 2/3rd of the length

For the left slipper, from the right edge, fold in a little more than 1/3rd of the rectangle and place a marker. Open the fold, use a 2-yard strand of yarn and make a running stitch along the very edge of the marked part taking care to catch only one loop.

Pull both ends to cinch. Do not cinch too tight or you will feel a lump in your slipper. Tie both ends to hold it in place and sew any opening shut working through the very edge and catching only 1 loop at a time, knot to secure.

Sew back to get your yarn near the marker, do not trim the excess yarn. We will come back to this part later after sewing the ankle side.

Right Slipper-Cinching Toe Side

Keep the rectangle textured side up. The toe side should be at the top.

A little more than 2/3rd

Easy Crochet Slippers

3. Start from the left side, make a running stitch along 2/3rd of the length

For the right slipper, from the left edge, fold in a little more than 1/3rd of the rectangle and place a marker. Cinch the left side this time and seam it just like you did with your left slipper.

Note: When you seam the ankle side or the back of your slipper, the seam will be worked 1/2 inch inwards along the top half to make it snug.

Fold the ankle side in the middle, align the top edges, using the yarn tail left, start seaming the ankle working 1/2 inch inside, work along a slanting line to hit the middle, and from there work along the very edge to join the 2 layers.

Make a couple of knots. The ankle seam will be a little to the side because of the way these slippers are shaped.

Easy Crochet Slippers

Closing the Toe Side- Left and Right Slipper

Turn the slipper right side out. The flap will fold to the right for the right slipper and to the left for the left slipper.

Now insert your foot into the slipper. If you are making it for someone else and the slipper is too small to fit, just insert the front of your foot.

Fold the flap over as far as possible and sew in place using the yarn tail left at the toe side. You can use a running stitch. Since tapestry needle is blunt you don't have to worry about poking your foot.

Easy Crochet Slippers

Finishing the Crochet Slipper

1. Sew on 2 or 3 buttons to the edge of the flap for embellishment. Repeat with the other slipper.

2. Weave in any tails left along the inner side of the slipper.

1.5 Hour Slipper

MATERIALS:

1. Size 6 Super Bulky Chenille yarn. Bernat Blanket yarn in colors Pale Gray and Merlot, and Bernat Baby Blanket yarn in color Overcast was used for the samples.

2. Red Heart Hygge Fur in color Cotton Tail for the edging

3. An N/P(10mm) hook for the main slipper and a K(6.5mm) hook for the fur trim

4. A big eye tapestry needle to weave in the ends

Easy Crochet Slippers

5. A locking stitch marker or a safety pin.

Finished Size

Note: Size refers to US shoe sizes. The slipper is designed to have 1/4-1/2 inch wiggle room.

Yardage

Each pair takes around 100 yards of the super bulky yarn. You can make 2 pairs from one skein of Bernat Blanket yarn of 220 yards.

Stitch Abbreviations

ch– chain

st– stitch

sc– single crochet

sl st– slip stitch

YO– yarn over

Easy Crochet Slippers

Gauge

7 sc sts and 7 Rows = 4 inches

Stitch Explanations

1. sc2tog: It is a decrease that joins 2 sts into one.

To work a sc2tog, insert your hook into the next st or space specified and pull up a loop, insert your hook into the next st and pull up a loop, YO and pull through all the 3 loops on your hook.

2. sc3tog: It is a decrease that joins 3 sts into one.

To work a sc3tog, *(insert your hook into the next st and pull up a loop), repeat from * 2 more times, YO and pull through all the 4 loops on your hook.

Pattern Notes

1. Sizes 5 to 9 are grouped together and sizes 10 to 12 are grouped together.

Easy Crochet Slippers

Sizes 5 to 9

With the bigger 10mm hook, ch 4.

Note: When you work 2 sc into the free loops of the foundation chain, work your first sc inserting your hook under one loop and the second one inserting hook under the junction of the current loop and next loop where they cross. This will make any hole left smaller.

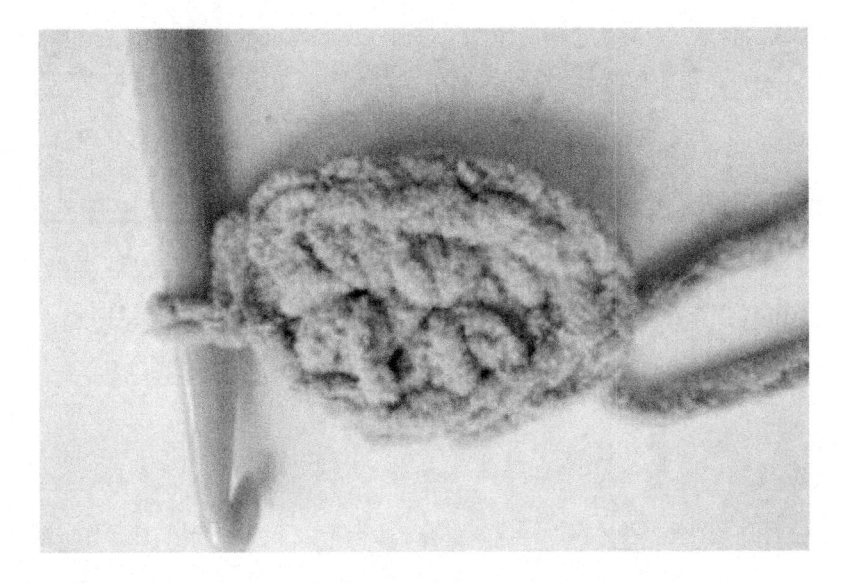

Round 1: 2 sc in 2nd ch from hook, 2 sc in next ch, 3 sc in last ch, pivot to work along the opposite side of the foundation chain as shown in pic 1 above, 2 sc in the first free loop of the foundation ch, 2 sc in the next free loop of the foundation ch, sl st to first sc, do not turn. —

Easy Crochet Slippers

———11 sc

Round 2: Ch 1 (does not count as a st), *(1 sc in next st, 2 sc in next st), repeat from * 4 more times, 1 sc in next st, do not sl st and do not turn.———16 sc

Notes

1. We will now start working in a spiral without sl stitching at the end of rounds.

2. We will place a marker in the first st of every round to keep track of the rounds. Every time you work a st into the marked st, move the marker up into the st you just worked to indicate the beginning of the new round.

Round 3: Sk the next ch(it looks like a st but is actually the beginning ch 1), 1 sc into the next sc, place a marker in this sc. 1 sc in next 15 sts until you work a sc in the st right before the marked one, do not sl st and do not turn.———16 sc

Easy Crochet Slippers

Round 4: 1 sc in the marked st, move the marker up, 1 sc in next 15 sts until you work a sc in the st right before the marked one, do not sl st and do not turn.———16 sc

Notes

1. Before you proceed any further, use your beginning tail to close any gaps at the toe side and weave in the rest of the tail.

2. At the end of each round, make sure to write down the number of rounds you have completed. It can be hard to count your rounds when you are working in a spiral.

Repeat Round 4 until you have completed 9 Rounds for size 5, 10 Rounds for sizes 6 and 7, 11 Rounds for size 8, and 12 Rounds for size 9.

Heel Side- Sizes 5 to 9

Easy Crochet Slippers

Row 1: Sl st to next marked st. You can now take off the marker. We won't be using it anymore. Ch 1, 1 sc in same st as ch 1, 1 sc in next 10 sts, turn——11 sc

Row 2 & 3: Ch 1, 1 sc in same st as ch 1, 1 sc in next 10 sts, turn. —— 11 sc

Row 4: Ch 1, 1 sc in same st as ch 1, 2 sc in next, 1 sc in 7 sts, 2 sc in next, 1 sc in last st, turn.——13 sc

Easy Crochet Slippers

Row 5: Ch 1, 1 sc in same st as ch 1, 1 sc in next 12 sts, turn. ——13 sc

Row 6: Ch 1, 1 sc in same st as ch 1, 2 sc in next, 1 sc in 3 sts, sc3tog across next 3 sts, 1 sc in next 3 sts, 2 sc in next, 1 sc in last st, turn.——13 sc

Row 7: Ch 1, 1 sc in same st as ch 1, 1 sc in next 12 sts, turn. Do not fasten off. ——13 sc

Seaming the Heel

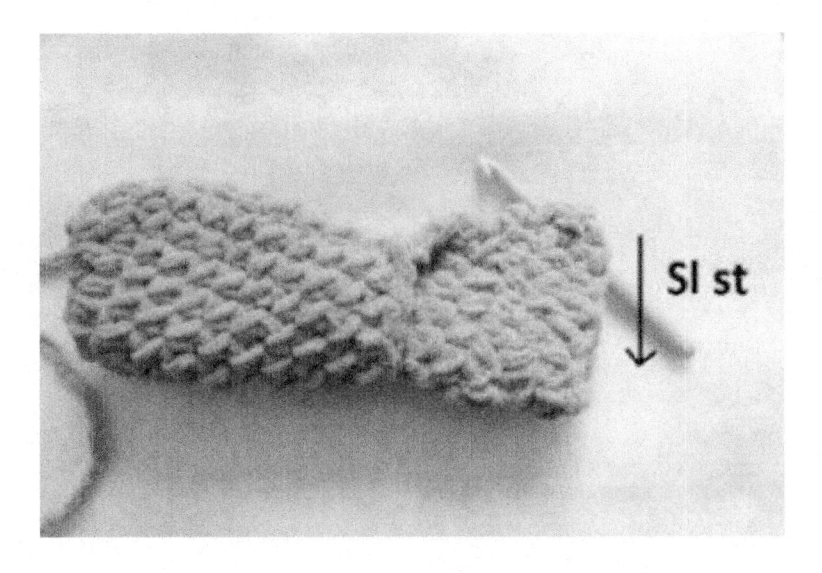

Easy Crochet Slippers

Now fold your last row in half and work a sl st seam on the inside of your slipper as shown in pic 4 above. Insert your hook only through the front loop of the front layer and the back loop of the back layer when you slip stitch. This will prevent bulk from forming at your seam. End with a sl st in the corner as shown in pic 5 above. Fasten off.

Working Around the Opening

Notes

1. While working the first round of sc sts around the opening.

2. When you work the first sc round, you can work over the yarn tail to weave it in.

Easy Crochet Slippers

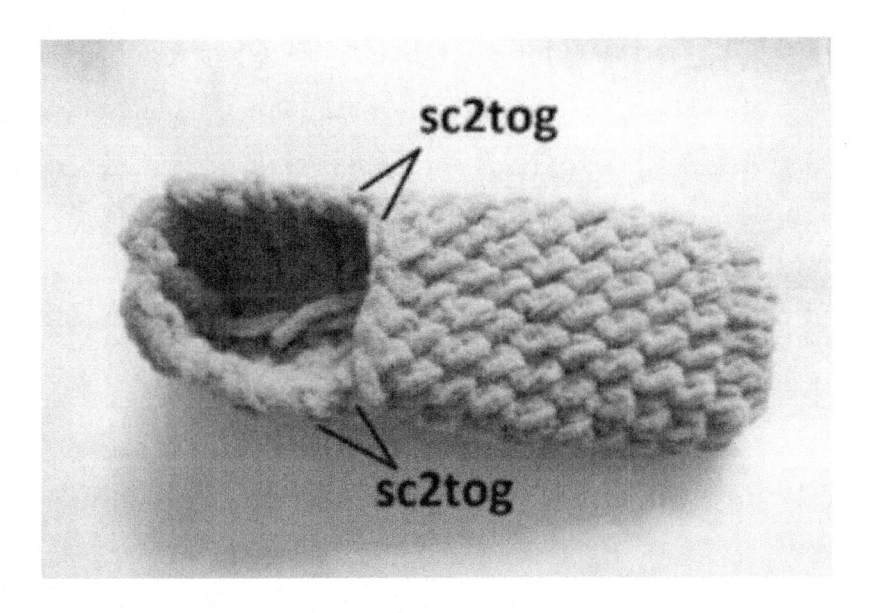

Round 1 (for sizes 5 to 8 only): With the bulky yarn, sl st to the back of the heel, ch 1 and work 21 sc sts around the opening with sc2tog at the junction between the heel and the toe side as shown in pic 7 above, sl st to the first sc, fasten off.———21 sc

Round 1 (for size 9): With the bulky yarn, sl st to the back of the heel, ch 1 and work 22 sc sts around the opening with sc2tog at the junction between the heel and the toe side as shown in pic 7 above, sl st to the first sc, fasten off. ———22 sc

Easy Crochet Slippers

Round 2(All 5 sizes): With the fur yarn and K(6.5mm) hook, sl st to the back of the heel, ch 1, working over the fur tail, 1 sc in same st as ch 1, 1 sc in each st across until you reach near the toe side where you worked the sc2tog, 2 sc into the sc2tog, 1 sc in each st until you reach the next sc2og, 2 sc into the sc2tog, 1 sc in each st across to end, sl st to first sc, do not turn.

Note: Now we will add more sts to make our fur edging fluffy.

Round 3: Ch 1, 2 sc in same st as ch 1, 2 sc in each st around, sl st to first sc, do not turn.

Round 4: Ch 1, sc2tog in the same st as ch 1 and next st, *(sc2tog across the next 2 sts), repeat from * to end, sl st to first sc, do not turn.

Rounds 5 & 6: Ch 1, 1 sc in same st as ch 1, 1 sc in next st and each st across to end, sl st to first sc, do not turn. Fasten off after Round 6.

Easy Crochet Slippers

Finishing the Slipper

Weave in any tails left. You just have to randomly weave in the fur yarn, and it will disappear into your work.

Sizes 10, 11 & 12

With the bigger 10mm hook, ch 4.

Note: When you work 2 sc into the free loops of the foundation chain, work your first sc inserting your hook under one loop and the second one inserting hook under the junction of the current loop and next loop where they cross. When working the third sc into the last loop, dig your hook a little deeper. This will close any hole.

Round 1: 2 sc in 2nd ch from hook, 2 sc in next ch, 3 sc in last ch, pivot to work along the opposite side of the foundation chain as shown in pic 8 above, 2 sc in the first free loop of the foundation ch, 3 sc in the next free loop, sl st to first sc, do not turn. ————12 sc

Easy Crochet Slippers

Round 2: Ch 1 (does not count as a st), *(1 sc in next st, 2 sc in next st), repeat from * 5 more times, do not sl st and do not turn.———18 sc

Notes

1. We will now start working in a spiral without sl stitching at the end of rounds.

2. We will place a marker in the first st of every round to keep track of the rounds. Every time you work a st into the marked st, move the marker up into the st you just worked to indicate the beginning of the new round.

Round 3: Sk the next ch (it looks like a st but is actually the beginning ch 1), 1 sc into the next sc, place a marker in this sc. 1 sc in next 17 sts until you work a sc in the st right before the marked one, do not sl st and do not turn.———18 sc

Round 4: 1 sc in the marked st, move the marker up, 1 sc in next 17 sts until you work a sc in the st right before the marked one, do not sl st and do not turn.———-18 sc

Easy Crochet Slippers

Heart & Sole Slippers

MATERIALS:

- 2 skeins of DK (light worsted)/ 8 ply yarn in Red (color A) and small amount of White (color B).

- 4.5 mm crochet hook

Easy Crochet Slippers

- 2 stitch markers

- tapestry needle to sew in the ends

- scissors.

GAUGE: 16 fpdc x 15 rounds = 10cm x 10cm (unstretched) = 4 inches x 4 inches

STITCHES AND ABBREVIATIONS (US TERMS):

ch: chain

sc: single crochet

hdc: half double crochet

dc: double crochet

fpdc: front post double crochet

bpdc: back post double crochet

st: stitch

yo: yarn over

Easy Crochet Slippers

slst: slip stitch

sk: skip

RS: right side

WS: wrong side

SPECIAL STITCHES:

bpdc2tog inv= invisible decrease back post double crochet= yo and insert hook from the back to the front around the post of the next 2 sts (at the same time) on the previous row. Complete as for regular dc.

How to change colors

Work the last st before changing colors till half, having 2 loops on hook, pick new color yarn and end the stitch, pulling the new color yarn through the 2 loops on hook.

Do not not cut yarns when changing colors, you can choose to work around the yarn not in use, or you can carry the unworked yarns across the back. Keep the tension of the strands not in use a little loose, to maintain elasticity.

Easy Crochet Slippers

To avoid long floats of yarn, you need to catch the yarn not in use.

INSTRUCTIONS

Work rounds 1- 5 the same for both left and right slippers!

Start with a magic ring.

Round 1: ch1, work 11 hdc into ring, join with sl st to top of first hdc. (11 sts)

Round 2: ch2, (1 dc into top of next st, 1fpdc around the same st as the dc just made), repeat around, join with sl st to top of first st. (22 sts)

Round 3: ch2, 1fpdc around each of next 4 sts, (1dc into top of next st, 1 fpdc around same st), 1 fpdc around next st, (1dc into top of next st, 1 fpdc around same st), 1 fpdc around each of next 8 sts, (1dc into top of next st, 1 fpdc around same st), 1 fpdc around next st, (1dc into top of next st, 1 fpdc around same st), 1 fpdc around each of next 4 sts; join with sl st to top of first fpdc. (26 sts)

Round 4: ch2, 1fpdc around each of next 5 sts, (1dc into top of next st, 1 fpdc around same st), 1 fpdc around next st, (1dc into top of next st, 1 fpdc around same st), 1 fpdc around each of next 10 sts, (1dc into top of next st, 1 fpdc around same st), 1 fpdc around next st, (1dc into top of next st, 1 fpdc around same st), 1 fpdc around each of next 5 sts; join with sl st to top of first fpdc. (30 sts)

Round 5: ch2, 1fpdc around each of next 6 sts, (1dc into top of next st, 1 fpdc around same st), 1 fpdc around next st, (1dc into top of next st, 1 fpdc around same st), 1 fpdc around each of next 12 sts, (1dc into top of next st, 1 fpdc around same st), 1 fpdc around next st, (1dc into top of next st, 1 fpdc around same st), 1 fpdc around each of next 6 sts; join with sl st to top of first fpdc. (34 sts)

Begin of Heart Pattern

Because the heart has an uneven number of stitches and the slippers

Easy Crochet Slippers

have an even number of sts in a round, the heart is not quite centered. One st is off.

(You have 1st more in main color on one side as on the other side of the heart.)

To make the slippers looking symmetrical when worn you will work the right slipper with the changes as seen below.

NOTE: Work rounds 6 - 13 as written in the pattern for the Left Foot with changes in parentheses for the Right Foot.

Round 6: ch2, with A 1fpdc in each of next 16 (17)sts, changing to B at last st, with B 1fpdc around next stitch changing to A when the st it's made till half; continue with A and work 1fpdc around each of next 17 (16) sts, sl st to top of first fpdc.

Round 7: With A ch2, work 1fpdc around each of next 15 (16) sts, changing to B at last st; with B 1fpdc around each of next 3 sts changing to A at last st, continue with A and work 1fpdc around each of next 16 (15)sts, sl st to top of first fpdc.

Round 8: With A ch2, work 1fpdc around each of next 14 (15)sts, changing to B at last st; with B 1fpdc around each of next 5 sts changing to A at last st, continue with A and work 1fpdc around each of next 15(14)sts, sl st to top of first fpdc.

Round 9: With A ch2, work 1fpdc around each of next 13 (14)sts, changing to B at last st; with B 1fpdc around each of next 7 sts changing to A at last st, continue with A and work 1fpdc around each of next 14 (13)sts, sl st to top of first fpdc.

Rounds 10-11: With A ch2, work 1 fpdc around each of next 12 (13)sts, changing to B at last st; with B 1 fpdc around each of next 9 sts changing to A at last st, continue with A and work 1 fpdc around each of next 13 (12) sts, sl st to top of first fpdc.

Round 12: With A work 1 fpdc around each of next 12 (13)sts, changing to B at last st; with B 1 fpdc around each of next 4 sts changing to A at last st, with A work 1 fpdc till half, change to B and finish the st with B; continues with B, work 1 fpdc around each of next 4 sts changing to A at last st, with A work 1 fpdc around each of next 13 (12) sts, sl st to top of first fpdc.

Easy Crochet Slippers

Round 13: With A ch2, work 1 fpdc around each of next 13 (14) sts, changing to B at last st; with B 1 fpdc around each of next 2 sts changing to A at last st, with A work 1 fpdc around each of next 3 sts, change to B at last st, with B 1 fpdc around each of next 2 sts changing to A at last st, with A work 1 fpdc around each of next 14 (13) sts, sl st to top of first fpdc. Cut yarn B.

Rounds 14: With A work 34 fpdc around, sl st to top of first fpdc.

THE GRAPH(S)

How to Read the Graph(s)

The 2 graphs are showing rounds 5- 14 in the written pattern.

Actually the 2 graphs are the same, the only thing that is different it's how you will read them:

The top graph is for the Left Foot. You will read the graph (beginning at the arrow) from bottom to top, from right to left.

The Bottom graph is for the Right Foot. You will read the graph

Easy Crochet Slippers

(beginning at the arrow) from bottom to top from left to right

Rounds 15-18: Repeat as round 14.

Note: It will be much easier to count the rounds/ rows on the wrong side. Count the ridges on the wrong side and write down to make the same for the second slipper.

(At the end of round 18 you will have 17 ridges on the wrong side.)

For larger slippers, continue until the desired length.

Cut yarn. Fasten off.

Start working in rows!

NOTE: ch 2 at beg of rows will count from now on as a hdc.

Left foot: Holding the piece with the back seam facing you count 14 sts from the back seam to the right, place a stitch marker into 14th st and a second stitch marker into the 22th st.

Easy Crochet Slippers

Right foot: Holding the piece with the back seam facing you count 13 sts from the back seam to the right, place a stitch marker into 13th st and a second stitch marker into the 21th st.

For both slippers you will have the stitch markers placed right above the heart, as seen in the picture below:

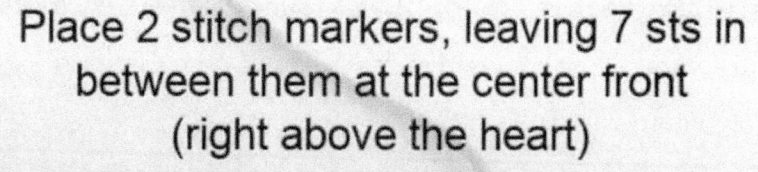

Place 2 stitch markers, leaving 7 sts in between them at the center front (right above the heart)

Easy Crochet Slippers

Next: For both slippers: Join yarn with a standing hdc into the first marked st. Continue to work row 1 below.

Row 1 Left Foot(RS): work 1 fpdc around each of next 13 sts, sk the joining seam below and work 1 fpdc around each of next 12 sts, 1 hdc into 2nd marked st, turn. (27 sts)

Row 1 Right Foot(RS): work 1 fpdc around each of next 12 sts, sk the joining seam below and work 1 fpdc around each of next 13 sts, 1 hdc into 2nd marked st, turn. (27 sts)

From here worked the same for both slippers!

Row 2 (WS): ch2, (count as hdc), 1 bpdc around each of next 25 sts, 1 hdc in top of standing hdc of previous round, turn. (27 sts)

Row 3 (RS): ch2, (count as hdc), 1 fpdc around each of next 25 sts, 1 hdc in top of ch2, turn. (27 sts)

Easy Crochet Slippers

Row 4 (WS): ch2, (count as hdc), 1 bpdc around each of next 25 sts, 1 hdc in top of ch2, turn.(27 sts)

Rows 5-11: Repeat as rows 3-4. (After finishing row 11 you will have 10 ridges, counted from where you began working in rows).

(For larger size, continue until you reach the desired length.)

Row 12 (WS): DECREASE ROW (you will decrease 2 sts) : ch2, 1 bpdc around each of next 10 sts, bpdc2tog inv, 1 bpdc around next st, bpdc2tog inv, 1 bpdc around each of next 10 sts, 1 hdc in top of ch2. (25 sts)

Last Row: ch2, 1fpdc around each of next 23 sts, 1 hdc in top of ch2. (25 sts).

Joining the sides at the Heel

Turn piece on the wrong side.

Ch1, join at heel the sides together by slip stitching through both top

Easy Crochet Slippers

loops of each side.

Don't fasten off! Slip stitch back to top. Ch 1 and turn piece on the right side again.

Continue to work the cuff around the foot opening:

The Cuff

Round 1: Work 34 or 36 hdc evenly spaced around the foot opening, sl st to top of first st.

For a larger opening work more sts, but the total number should be a multiple of 2!

Round 2: ch3, sk 1 st, *1 fpdc around next st, ch1, sk 1 st*, repeat around from * to *, sl st with B to top of first fpdc.

Round 3: with B ch2, 1 fpdc around first skipped hdc 2 rounds below, ch1, sk next fpdc, *1 fpdc around next skipped hdc 2 rounds below, ch1, sk next fpdc*, repeat from * to * around, sl st with A to top of first fpdc.

Round 4: with A ch2, 1fpdc around first skipped fpdc 2 rounds below, ch1, sk next fpdc, *1 fpdc around next skipped fpdc 2 rounds below, ch1, sk next fpdc*, repeat from * to * around, at the last repeat don't ch 1 anymore before slip stitching to top of first fpdc.

Cut yarn. Fasten off. Weave in the ends.

Shell Slipper

MATERIALS:

1. Worsted weight yarn. Caron United in color Soft Grey Heather was used for the sample.

2. Hook G (4.25mm)

Easy Crochet Slippers

Size

Small (Fits US sizes 5 & 6): Slipper is 9 inches long

Medium (Fits US sizes 7 & 8): Slipper is 9 1/2 inches long

Large (Fits US sizes 9 & 10): Slipper is 10 inches long

Gauge

Working in hdc crochet, 16 sts and 8 1/2 Rows = 4 inches

Stitch Abbreviations

The pattern is written in standard American terms.

ch- chain

sc- single crochet

dc- double crochet

sl st- slip st

sk- skip

Easy Crochet Slippers

Stitch Explanation

Shell: 5 dc worked into the same st.

sc2tog (single crochet decrease): This will join 2 sts into one. To work a sc2tog, [insert your hook into the next st and pull up a loop]2 times, yarn over and pull through all the loops on your hook.

Pattern

Note: Sizes Small and Medium are grouped together and size Large is given separately.

Easy Crochet Slippers

Sizes Small and Medium

Note: The end of the round stitch counts include the chains between the stitches as well.

Round 2: Ch 3(counts as a dc here and throughout), 2 dc in same st as ch 3, ch 1, sk 1, 1 sc in next, *(ch 1, sk 1, 3 dc in next, ch 1, sk 1, 1 sc in next), repeat from * 2 times until you end with a sc in the same st as beginning ch-3, ch 1, sl st to the top of beginning ch-3. Do not turn.——— 24 sts

Easy Crochet Slippers

Round 3: 1 sc in next dc, place a marker in the sc you just made, *(ch 1, sk the next dc and ch 1, 3 dc in next sc, ch 1, 1 sc in the middle dc of the next 3dc group, ch 1, sk next dc and ch 1, 4 dc in next sc, ch 1, 1 sc in the middle dc of the next 3dc group), repeat from * and after you work 4dc in the last sc st, ch 1, sl st to first marked sc. Do not turn.———-26sts

Note: You will be skipping dc sts to work a shell into the sc.

Round 4: Ch 3, 4 dc in same st as ch-3, ch 1, 1 sc in middle dc of next 3dc group, ch 1, shell in next sc, ch 1, 1 sc in 3rd dc of next 4 dc group, ch 1, shell in next sc, ch 1, 1 sc in middle dc of next 3dc group, ch 1, shell in next sc, ch 1, 1 sc in 3rd dc of next 4 dc group, ch 1, sl st to top of beginning ch 3. Do not turn.——————32 sts (4 shells)

Round 5: Sl st into next dc, 1 sc in next, place a marker in the sc you just made, ch 1, shell in next sc, *(ch 1, 1 sc in middle dc of next shell, ch 1, shell in next sc), repeat from * and after shell in the last sc, ch 1, sl st to first marked sc. Do not turn———32 sts(4 shells)

Round 6: Ch 3, 4 dc in same st as ch-3, *(ch 1, 1 sc in middle dc of next shell, ch 1, shell in next sc), repeat from * and after 1 sc in 3rd dc of the last shell, ch 1, sl st to top of beginning ch 3. Do not turn.———— ————32 sts (4 shells)

Round 7: Repeat Round 5.

Round 8: Repeat Round 6. Do not turn and do not fasten off.

Middle and Back of the Slipper

Easy Crochet Slippers

Notes

1. This part is worked in rows and then the backside is seamed to close the slipper.

2. The beginning ch2 does not count as a stitch in the following rows.

Row 1: Working in back loops only, ch 2, 1 hdc in same st as ch 2, 1 hdc in next 20 sts, turn.———21 sts

Easy Crochet Slippers

Row 2: Working in front loops only, ch 2, 1 hdc in same st as ch 2, 1 hdc in next 20 sts, turn.———21 sts

Repeat the above 2 rows until your shoe measures 6 1/2 inches for size Small and 7 inches for size Medium.

Increase Rows

Note: Maintain the sequence of working into the back and front loops. On the right side of the shoe, you will work in back loops, and on the wrong side, you will work into the front loops.

Easy Crochet Slippers

Increase Row 1:Ch 2, 1 hdc in same st as ch 2, 2 hdc in next, 1 hdc in each st until 2 sts are left, 2 hdc in next, 1 hdc in last st. turn.———23 sts

Repeat the above increase row 2 more times to end in 27 sts and turn.

Next Row: Ch 2, 1 hdc in same st as ch 2, 1 hdc in next 26 sts, turn.———27 sts

Last Row: Ch 1, 1 sc in same st as ch 1, 1 sc in next 3 sts, 1 hdc in next 4 sts, 1 sc in next 2 sts, (sc2tog)3 times, 1 sc in next 2 sts, 1 hdc in next 5 sts, 1 sc in last 4 sts.———24 sts.

Border Around the Slipper

You will now work 2 rounds around the opening of the slipper with a few decreases thrown in. This will make your slippers snug and keep it from falling off your feet. You will be working across row ends for the most part and will have to distribute your sc as evenly as possible.

Easy Crochet Slippers

Round 1: Sl st to the back seam, ch 1, sc2tog, work sc evenly around the slipper with 5 decreases (sc2tog), 1 at the back, 1 on either side and 1 at each of the corners of the toe top as shown. Sl st to the 1st sc, do not turn.———48(52) sts

Round 2: Ch 1, 1 sc in same st as ch 1, *(sk 1 st, 1 sc in next, 1 sc in the previous skipped st), repeat from * to end and sl st to the first sc. Fasten off and weave in the tails.

Your slipper is now ready to keep you warm and comfy!

Printed in Great Britain
by Amazon